OF LOVE, LONGING & OTHER POEMS

NIDHI RANA

INDIA • SINGAPORE • MALAYSIA

ISBN 979-8-89067-608-5

To the ones

who gave me spirit and the vision

to absorb the essence of light

and sing the songs of life

with love!!

Contents

NOSTALGIA

The Prelude

It gives me immense joy to bring this book to you and I hope it's a pleasure for you to read it. These poems are my meditations on love, life and all that has made me. Some poems have been inspired from my own experiences, others have come through empathy and understanding of your life. And then there are many that have come out of my imagination, stirred by a word here or a thought there. Though I am an eager reader of books too but life itself has been one great book and has given me the opportunity to take as much as I could. There are times I have taken the lesson and at others I have simply been blown away by the wind, destined to go astray, to not find 'that' pearl of wisdom that the universe intended. I have learnt some and much still eludes me but I want to keep my quest on, to find what life is and how one must go through it. I sing of what has been lost or found, carrying echoes of those before me. Have you ever seen a kite flying high in the sky on a beautiful sunny day? That's exactly how I feel when I write and this feeling is a pure beauty. There have been times when I have simply stared at the blank page before me for hours with right words eluding me and the emotion bursting my heart to be let out. I have fiddled with words and spent nights with them when the world slept lost in a dream. Riddled with the challenges that a poet must undertake, the provocations caused to my sensibilities, the defiance of the norms or submission to my own idiosyncrasies, whatever has made me, has brought forth this book you have in your hand. All I can say is that it has been an amazing journey and I wish it is so for you as well.

Happy Reading!!

LOVE & LONGING

Museum of Innocence

In search of lost time,

I am the vagabond

who visits each crevasse

of memory

where,

a kiss was more than a kiss

and a promise was life incarnate

and a tear was a loss so keen, the whole world could not

replace.

A feeling was a treasure- guarded and sealed

and,

A touch was the unabashed desire that explored without

guilt.

Now,

those kisses, promises, tears, feelings, desires,

all line up on the glass shelves

of the museum of innocence

that I unknowingly built.

Now and then,

I buy myself the ticket

to revisit the labyrinthine galleries

and consume the love

sediments of which

I still find stuck,

imprinted,

frozen in time,

hanging in the stale air.

Once More

I want to hold your hand once more,

as we walk in the red moonlight,

when the spring leaves rustle

in rhythm with the breeze of silky night.

I want to look into your eyes once more,

and hear the breath that warmed me,

when the ash moon cast its long-lost shadows,

playing desire between branches of the tree.

I want once more to smell the visions with you,

that wafted from busy houses on the lonely street,

when we wove impossible dreams of a life together,

How our souls in the darkness of night did meet!

My Soul at Night

The night carried
the sound of a lone wind chime
tinkling, making noise.

I don't know
if it was the sound of
a cracked bell,
a broken heart
or a sad song of love.

It carried me to the by-lanes,
old, left years ago,
in a faded book of memories.

The chime
revived on my lashes
the forgotten burden of loss.

I looked at the moon

hanging sadly on the branch

in my window.

I haven't been able to forget you.

Do you sometimes think of me too?

The Rain Last Night

The rain streamed all night

in a seamless harmony

speaking in a language

only the lovers could appreciate.

It asked to be embraced

quivering inside for

togetherness and satiety

as it balanced itself

on the edge of a promise

not feigned

but real

made to be kept

endlessly.

God

What must God look like?

Majestic in His benevolence

Fierce in His justice

Apocalyptic in His anger

Angelic in His smile

Austere in His desire

Hesitant in His anxiety

Formidable in His fear

and

Human in His love!

Unto My Soul

As the picking wind slowly swings through the trees
the hanging bells dance and sing mayhem melodies,
I sing songs of you . . .

As the clouds gather darkening the apocalyptic skies,
and the drip-drop drizzle knocking at my window spies,
I think thoughts of you . . .

As the birds run twittering against the rushing rain,
finding their nests among the reeds and wild cane,
I dream dreams of you . . .

When the rain starts to splatter hard against the pane,
blurring the contours of the world outside,
I move inside reaching unto my soul,
with your songs, your thoughts, your dreams!

If Only

Hearing you smile over the phone,

miles across,

oceans apart,

I could taste the times past.

I thought back to

the days full of golden sun,

suffused with silver smiles,

nights lit by the strawberry moon,

the sighs lasting awhile.

And now

I can only wish,

pray . . .

If only my eyes could feel you once

If only my hands could touch you again

I would fill the vial of my being,

with your presence

quite enough to live

the rest of my life through!

An Autumn Rendezvous

Standing at the ridge of the mountain,

I looked down into the gorge and its deep,

the pines murmured their own hill-songs,

and our song of love writ loud on my heart's leap.

The autumn breeze lent its smell to the ageless stones,

we walked, till where the path cleaves,

breeding mood, sighing love, making music,

hidden beneath the yellowing leaves.

By the burbling waters of the brook,

I found a kiss resting on your lips,

stealing it slowly away from you,

pines whispered, nodding, rubbing their needle tips.

The verdant fields, uneven and terraced,

lined the canvas as far as I could see,

we sat back smelling the memories from the past,

Our autumn rendezvous colored with love of you and me!

How We Loved!

I look at the moon

and think of you

and the love we had

Oh! How we loved!

I think of the nights

when under the star-spangled sky

our fingers together traced the constellations,

and made it a home,

a world away from world.

And I have not forgotten

the warm nook of your shoulders

where I rested my head

but

howsoever I try

I cannot recall

your face

and yet

I see you in all that is love!

Is that how time tricks?

or

Is it my heart tired of the effort of rebuilding the lines of
your face?

I cannot know

but

I keep wandering in the maze of old times lived!

I Once Saw Love

Did you ever see love?
I once did!

Dove-eyed, it sat on a branch
among the wild, red flowers,
showering liquesce smile
raining its heady arrows,
on a maiden who sat in the shadows
enwrapped in the arms of her lover.

It was love in her sweet surrender,
when the lines between the two blurred into nothing.

It was love when she cast away her masks,
and he lay there as her mirror,
reflecting her cubbyholes,
Oh! How he loved her all.

With the masks cast away,
her beauty he could see,
without any pretensions,

with no conceit,

she entered his heart,

and for eternity it was to be!

I once saw love!!

My Spectrum

My black is
the black of the night
that whispers your dreams into my sleep.

My white is the one
that colours the morning mist
gathering softly around your breath,
waking me conscious.

You are the yellow
of the warm winter noon
that overwhelms my senses
with the oozy fragrance of ripened berries.

My red is the red of the roses you send me
whose thorns unwittingly prick my fingers
making me sometimes taste the salt of blood.

My blue is
that of the midnight skies
when I melt in your arms
moored on the shores of lands unknown.

You are the colours

that fill the spectrum of my being

the hues of

the warmth and the pain

in my existence.

One Evening

They sat by the lake
as the sky shed its brighter blue
to wear the black of the night.

Rocks slept under their feet,
as she got lost in his story.

He was a great storyteller,
telling tales of the worlds yet unknown to her.

Pointing to the silhouette of the low hills
beyond the lake,
he said that it was raining there.

She imagined their life together
on one such evening
when by the fireplace
he would play his guitar
to the tune of the falling rain.

And later she would read Rumi,

may be Faiz,

feeding their passion

and their undying love!!

God in Love

As I rocked my year-old daughter to sleep,

crooned into the deep of my arm,

I looked long at her,

innocent and vulnerable,

in her little baby's charm.

I gazed fondly into her twinkling eyes

who focused into mine

searching for the angel of sleep.

And I couldn't help but opine:

'This is what God must look like in love!'

Roses

Walking barefoot

on the grass

in the garden

with our gazes melting

on the Iceberg and the Sun God roses,

little by little

our love made the spring arrive!

The birds twittered at our shy smiles

resplendent with the colours of the season.

Our gentle steps treading

to the beat of our fluttering hearts.

Holding your hand

I knew

I could swerve by destiny.

I could,

at that moment,

look into the eyes of a God

and live through eternity

only to be yours forever!

Savage Hearts

Existing in the transience of a happy moment,

we sat by the lurching blue sea,

our feet foam-covered,

splashing in the moist shade of a canopy.

Casting long shadows,

standing on the white sands

we wove a coral love,

in the invisible fabric of the reef's white bands.

Our laughter all mixed

with the salt sprinkled across the sky

I heard green delight of the deep

with the gulls rested on the waves rising high.

We left our footprints embedded,

imprinted on the time that plays clever,

our savage hearts found love,

living from nothingness to forever!

Sweet Nothings

As the evening breeze,

gently soughs through trees,

the hanging chimes tinkle,

singing unsung melodies.

I long for you,

I want you home!

I hear the car in the drive, roar,

your muffled steps up the stairs,

and I run breathless to the door.

The hug,

the stolen kiss,

your shoes on the rug,

Your eyes my bliss!

The hot cup of tea,

the humdrum chatter,

the little world of you and me.

Could it be any better?

The feel of your rough skin,

as you pull me into you,

the light peck on your chin,

I love how we find our love anew.

The sweet sweet nothings

we together taste each day

in the newness of the monotony,

we keep falling in love every way!!

The Ghosts

The ghosts alive,

rise out of

the graves that breathe

inside me.

Their dance cultic,

in a ritual,

to restore the past,

but their ecstasy evades me

and I look ahead

towards the future

consigning them back

to their graves.

Did I not write an epitaph:

'Dear Love,

Rest in Peace?'

Our Love

Our love

has become

a fading fragment

in my memory

adamant

to hold on to

the ruins,

a part already erased

irretrievably lost

ravaged by time

like the Bamiyan Buddhas.

The remainder,

the residual char,

lodged desolate

in my head

as I

stagger between

sanity and madness.

Lost Time

Passing across the bridge

above the river,

all the lost time

came to me

in a procession of memory.

A time

that gushed away

as soon

like the water underneath,

shining its counterfeit gold

in the morning sun

winking at me,

burbling.

I wonder

at the pranks

the people can play

and the jest

the time can be.

Let Us Dissolve in This Rain

Let us dissolve in this rain

seep into the earth

and rise again

as trees that adorn the forest,

evaporate from their leaves

become clouds,

fall in surrender

over the mountains,

and as streams flow down

to meander lazily through the terrain,

reach the flatlands,

flood the ocean

become brine

and sleep inside the wild oyster

undisturbed

as a rare pearl

until recovered by the pearl diver.

NOSTALGIA

The Echo

The mango tree
stood tall and green,
quite as old as her-
my old great granny,
her each word love
led my heart astir.

Canopied noons
under the
blooming summer tree,
the fragrance of her tales,
kept me quite
as busy, as carefree.

Each wrinkle,
every crease,
held a story untold,
awe-struck,
the tree and I,
heard them unfold.

She spun

enchanting fables

reading from the book of her life,

moving narratives,

of love and loss,

of lessons she had learnt from strife.

Her fingers incessant

worked through raw cotton

on the wheel,

fabric of our being

wanted more,

waiting fervently at her heel.

Absorbing her patience,

the tree and I

lived happily our days,

but little did we know then,

of fate, of God,

and His many unknown ways.

Alone we now sit,

through the warm, lonely days,

missing her voice, her stories,

the echo of which stays!!

The Letter

There was some charm

in the feel of

the blue inland letter

in your hand

with your name written

in a drag of emotion

in blue ink

of a nibbed pen,

which carried the aroma

of the long journey

it had made

through letter boxes of

dank post offices

to reach you

and speak to you in human words

of love, pain, desire, anguish

and myriad sentiments

felt inside the heart.

My Hospital Room's Window

As I looked out of

my hospital room's large glass window,

I knew

that

all the whats,

the whens,

the hows,

the ifs and the buts

had become lame,

because the winter had already set in,

and there wasn't enough time to wait for the spring

that stood just around the corner!

Distances

I woke up because of the commotion.

Steps shuffling through the sanitized corridors

had woken me from a fitful sleep

I quickly forgot the lounge chair that had served me well.

My attention fast zeroed in on the men wearing white.

I was alone,

waiting outside,

while my father lay in the ICU.

There was no one I could speak with

in real,

A distance call does not count.

Now, does it?

My sister is in the US of A

great place,

of Silicon Valleys,

and American Dreams,

I agree,

but far,

if I wanted to reach her,

or for her to reach me,
this very hour.

I almost ran to the doctor,
Maybe I had slept too long.
Bottles of medicines passed by me
carried on speedy steps.
I needed to know
if my father was alright.
The doctor looked at me
Sadly
or was it accusingly?
Perhaps, he was just exhausted.
"His heart is sinking,
pulse non-committal,
we've put him on life-support
you can call your family."

Family?
I thought:
I am his family
and he's mine.

Just then the nurse called him in

with hasty words

and all alone

I stared into nothingness,

thinking of the distances

that lives suffer.

The Loss

Years ago,

there was a tree I planted.

In time, new leaves sprouted

its shoots grew

and were soon branching out to my window.

I had seen it grow,

bloom,

into a colossal presence in my life.

Each morning

I opened my eyes to see its green.

I loved it

and he knew it too.

For I had felt how he bent itself here and there

when I neared it,

touched it.

And then one day

I was made to leave for some place.

When I got home

it wasn't the home I had left-

my tree had been cut,

rooted out.

They said, 'It was wild.'

I had become rootless.

The emptiness gnawed at me.

And then,

I got married

and

slowly

forgot all about it.

Now,

he often comes to me

as the fragrance of

a hallowed memory.

The Mountain

Outside my window it stood
regal and solemn, in its silence.
Down at that table
its presence
impossible to ignore.

Other peaks too ranged across my horizon
but this one was different.
Its ancient soul called to me.

On many summer noons
I imagined its chirs,
their rustling needles
singing forgotten, primeval songs.

In the rains,
inaccessible, distant,
it lay fog-enshrouded
surreal to my world.

On the grey, winter nights,
its white, ice-bound desolation
lent to my sleep
some hallowed, snowy dreams.

When spring blossomed
clumsy and wild,
it was a riot of colours.
its heady fragrances, sickening sweet,
imagined in my head.

My mind races back to that house
in the hills
the table where I sat
and looked long at it.

Then we moved away.

That house,
that place,
that mountain,
have all lived in my memory,
in the mazy folds of my head.

Would that my matured years

lead me somehow

to the paths

I left untraversed

in childhood!

Old Age

I want to visit the by-lanes

of childhood once again

where darkness too could fire my imagination.

Ghosts, ghouls, phantoms, trolls,

came to life then

in infinite stories I wove,

and our dancing fingers

in the flickering light

of the candle

made giant specters on the wall

wakening sleeping giants

out of their slumber.

And my sister's touch in the night

made me jump out of myself

making fear but a game.

Now,

my heart has slowed

missing its beats,

my children keep excitement out of my reach

lest I should have a heart attack

and die.

The night bulb is left switched on,

so I don't fumble or fall

in the dark.

Though my fingers tingle,

I can't really dance them,

and fears rise out of the sinews of light.

Where Are My Wilds?

Once upon a time
beyond this ancient banyan tree
the savage, untamed nature laughed,
running amuck and free.
There, weed-flowers bloomed
violet, pink, yellow and blue
creepers girdled the Bamboos' green,
vibrant, wild brush-strokes of God,
clearly seen.

Now, I see manicured lawns
for as far as my eye heads,
green fresh-mowed grass
nurseries of flowers neatly cultured in beds,
gurgling metal-mermaids,
spouting docile streams of water are heard,
I can see the hand of man at work.

The reckless, untended wilderness is no more,
my muse sits back sad and sighs,
unhappy, she murmurs, "Where are my wilds?
For there's nothing that invokes my soul,
this civilization has brought man to his own fall."

The Rain

Rain tap-danced around me
while I sat motionless, parked,
listening to the pleuvisaud.

Cadences of the pitter-patter
beat a solemn tattoo on the car roof.
The violent strumming knocked gently
at a door of childhood.

The heavy monsoon rain
made little streams out of our streets
and we, as children, waded in those waters
getting drenched unto our soul.
We giggled, sang and danced,
even with mother's reproof
that waited back home.

Suddenly, coming to the moment,
I look longingly at the drumming water,
I want to jump out,
live this second.

The rain dramatically took a slight pause

out of my reverie,

out of the car,

I stepped inside my office,

and smiled back at

the present and the past!!

Dusk Games

The street sat surrounded

by the identical two-storeyed houses,

and we played

the dusk games

till the sumptuous smells

of a home-cooked meal

wafted into the air

filling our stomachs

with a hunger

only a child knows well.

And then,

our mothers called us inside.

with our bellies full,

we slept to her kisses,

slipping easily into a sleep,

filled with fairy dreams.

Now,

I see my daughters sleep the sleep

I had once known,

and remember

fragrance of the hand

that caressed my hair

affectionately

and tenderness of gentle lips

that kissed me goodnight.

My Lost Home

The war has ravaged

my city,

my people,

my home.

Enemy's hatred

plunders through the streets

as my people hide silently

behind broken walls.

Children die in gardens

bombed, besieged.

dead bodies rot beyond recognition

waiting to be buried by a loved one.

I helplessly watch the gore,

as I stealthily trudge my path

to become an exile,

to seek asylum

in a place yet unknown to me.

All that was mine

shall live inside me

in a broken part of my heart

as I take refuge

in another land

as an 'other'.

And forever shall

my displaced self

long for the home

lost forever to me.

The Traveller

I travel the world

and

come back home

to find my place

anew.

I have new eyes

that once again see

the photos forgotten

on the frayed walls.

I have new ears

that hear the laughter

from yesteryears

of the children

long grown and gone.

The nose smells

the aroma of

mother's cooking

that wafted

from the kitchen,

years ago.

The tongue tastes

memories,

and the sadness

they bring,

to mushroom nostalgia

within.

And my skin

tanned and old

feels the rush of the years

gone by

and wears signs of

the years untold.

The Night Rain

As the room darkens slowly

and the rain

fills the night,

the petrichor

rising from

the drenched soil

wakes something within

hidden under

the layers of time.

The earth's aroma

carries me

to the lanes of childhood

to the carefree,

beloved hours,

when

to the sound

of the falling rain

my mother told me stories

of sun and moon and kings and dragons,

and lay me down to sleep.

Nostalgia

There is something about the old houses,

now vacant and standing lost to time

that haunts me, pulling me to them.

The derelict walls echo their silence to the world.

But there lives a home in me,

where I can still hear the laughter around the dinner table,

I can still smell the bread and taste the wine.

The nostalgia of the needs of a life,

happy mostly,

only sometimes strained by strife.

I can still see the boy, who sang out loud in the kitchen,

curious about what baked in the oven.

I can still see the little girl, who pirouetted in the living
room,

practicing hours for the school concert.

I can still see the excited children weaving tales around
the fireplace,

sleep fairy dancing right above their eyelids.

I can still feel the amber warmth,

Of my lost home,

displaced in a time warp.

Oh! The nostalgia of a never-ending, simple tenderness,

of a family that now lives only in my memory!!

Sleep

In my half-awake, half-trance state of sleep

I long for a sleep inside my sleep

deeper, sounder

where even dreams cannot penetrate,

an opiate sleep without interruptions

white-noised

such that I do not exist

or remain oblivious that I do,

and be the air that stands

suspended, frozen, still,

inside a locked cell,

bringing to a halt

my torturous agonies

my unconscious vulnerabilities

such that

my insomniac affliction

gives way to peace,

a peace that may pervade my being

invisible to time

like the calm after a storm.

In the Silence of the Night

In the silence of the night

sip by sip

I slurp noisily

my coffee

and taste poem after poem.

I drink the words

that ring of

tenderness and commiseration,

desire and despair

affections and anxiety

and let the aroma permeate

into my blood

become a life

that I need to birth.

I bring forth new worlds

and numberless faces

never before seen.

SUFI SOUL

The Nomad

The nomad

is no(t)-mad

to wander

the winding paths

in the hills

alone,

but seeks fare

for his flock

and vies for

the mountains

with snow-molded crowns

that watch

from the horizon.

His strong arms

carry the tender lambs,

that are too weak to walk

on their trotters.

His vehement heart

carries

the impassioned image

of his home

he left

somewhere near

the snowline.

The fire

kindled at night,

his custodian,

keeps him warm

and wary

of lurking wolves

that pounce

out of the dark

and carry

the bleating ewe away

into the jungle.

His lone tunes

nostalgic

long for the flock

he left behind-

the loving arms,

the baby hands!

He walks

and he waits

for

when the snow melts

his bohemian feet

calloused,

would carry him back

to the hearth

that warms his soul

after he has roamed

up to the dreary foothills

to journey back

to his Eden,

and

his rhapsody

alive

ringing within him.

Faith

I tie my faith
around the branches
of the sacred tree
outside the temple.
The red of the thread
bleeds in rain
and dashes my hopes
to dust.
But I go around the tree
circumambulating
watering, resurrecting,
the drained thread
with hope.

Last Night

Last night

the wind woke me up

as it played pell-mell

on the mosquito net

when I lay sleeping

under the open sky

in the courtyard

of our summer house.

On the horizon

the silhouettes of the eucalyptuses

swayed wildly

dallying with

the squally current of air.

The moon had hidden

behind the clouds

ashen in the purple sky.

Inertia of the sleep

prevented me from getting up

and moving inside

to the quietness

of my room.

Gridlocked on my charpoy

I heard the nature

breathe above me.

The clamour outside,

the silence within,

and the fragrance of

the eucalyptus blooms

blended in with the scent of

freshly-planted paddy in the fields,

awakened my spirit

to a deeper consciousness

and experience oneness

with the spirit of the universe.

Running Out of Time

I looked at the tree,

in the middle of winter,

which stood naked

and shorn.

Once the spring arrives

and the sun shines,

it shall forget this state of bareness,

the *déshabillé*,

and rejoice

in the here and now

of its bloom.

Why then,

is it

that my human mind

does not

let go of the past pains?

Or,

forget the losses incurred?

Or

Why does my heart

cling to sorrows
I have learnt to hide from myself?

Tied and trapped,
I am held hostage
in this mental tumult.

I am running out of time!
Where is my spring?

For the Days Passed By

As the honeyed nostalgia fills me

for the days passed by,

I wonder,

how short this life is a-while

to do and die.

Just the day before, so it seems,

did we all together play,

from the twittering mornings,

through the warm, sweaty noon,

till the sun went down, all exhausted, to croon.

Hide 'n seek,

sneak-a-peek,

hopscotch, touch and go;

our play entwined with the boughs

of the grove backyard

and our laughter- all excited, aglow.

I remember the blue tractor

that sat rusty,

brooding in the courtyard,

its noisy exhaust,

its bumpy rides,

haunt me still.

How my feet ache

to race across the furrowed fields,

to take a dip in the river

that meandered through the village,

by the old water mill.

Sometimes, I long

for time to reverse.

For moments to return,

I whine, I groan.

But I know too

the time not stops, but just goes on!

Ah then!

On moments so well lived,

is there a need to moan?

All at Once

As a child
I lay on the ground
and loved to look at
the eagles freewheeling
across the blue expanse
of the sky.
The winter sun
and the world around me
stood still,
calm, almost meditating,
as I watched them float
far above me.

Now, when I am old
and lost in nothingness,
and days flit away unnoticed,
I long for those afternoons
where I was
the sunshine and the sky,
the eagle and the little girl,
the peace and the flight,
everything
all at once!

The Old Woman

The old woman

sat on a rusted, green bench

in a forgotten corner

of the park.

She sat

nodding to herself,

her shaky hands resting

on a walking stick.

She lived in the last house

on our street

all alone.

Suddenly,

her rheumy eyes lit up.

Her indulgent smile

made me glance

in the direction she gazed.

A pack of children

noisy and squealing

poked their curious sticks

into a shallow puddle
left by the morning rain.
In no time,
one landed
right in the middle of the muddy pool
splashing euphoria around.
Soon,
others followed his lead,
spreading sounds of riotous glee.

I wondered--
whatever she was thinking?
Did she think of her children
settled now in faraway lands?
or,
Did she think of her own childhood,
that lived in the nostalgia of a past,
which now seemed too far-fetched?
May be,
she wasn't thinking at all.

With her fond smile,
She might just be picking something
to savour in her lonely hours.
If she had grandkids waiting for her by the door,

tonight, at bedtime

they would have feasted on a tale

of brats who jumped in plashets!

The Stranger

Sunken eyes,

hollowed-out cheeks

I didn't know the stranger in front of me

but something made me touch his dimpled old chin.

I searched for signs of life

and at last, I did see him smile,

weak but infectious,

spreading from his lips to mine.

I implored the God within me,

if it was possible to rewind our story a bit,

to let me live the times past just one more time.

Is it insanity?

Or just a plea to stay sane?

His uneven gaze settled on me,

I smiled into his eyes.

Defeated, I asked myself,

Is this what life comes down to?

The old and the young,

then the young and the old,

the roles reversed,

traversed over time,

living through the unending cycles of birth and death.

Nidhi Rana 87

Writing My Own Story

I sat in my garden

watching the yellow winter

tip-toeing along the wall.

The warm sun

shining, and playful

in my daughter's restless hair.

Unmindful of the sun,

her tiny frame

fluttered impishly

after the blue-winged butterflies.

My little dog,

sedate and snoring

slept by the leg of my chair,

the mellow afternoon beauty lost to that sleepyhead.

Having lost the story somewhere,

I closed the book in my hands,

and took in the winter, the sun, the flutters, the snores.

Making the perfect moment,

a part of me,

writing my own story ---

A story called life!

After the Rain

After the rain
when the clouds parted awhile,
my eye caught a pack of little kids
playing at a mile.

In the muddy puddles of water,
they were dancing and prancing,
their teeny-weeny clothes
getting wet in their fancying.

They sat around in circles
with broken twigs in their hands,
urging forward the paper boats
sending thrill amongst their bands.

The trusting smiles on their lips
with curiosity shining in eyes,
searching something,
and suddenly it all makes them look wise.

And if you wonder,

let me tell you,

it is nothing much

just a tadpole swimming through,

even a wriggling earthworm would do.

They love it all-

all that seems nothing to a critical adult eye,

the ancient wisdom,

only in their innocence does lie.

The beauty that goes unnoticed,

they see it all,

look how they become one with the divine,

exactly where the adults fall.

Just see how easy they make it look,

what we grown-ups keep striving for,

kids walk the path of wisdom,

while we keep knocking at the door.

Seeking the unknown,

we remain quite afar,

not knowing, divine is within

and it is what we all are!

Nidhi Rana 91

Taking the Plunge

Through the mesh of my door,

I looked outside,

listening to the tales

resonating in silence of the night,

the darkness that had lulled everyone to sleep.

I was awake,

picturing the characters,

birthing into being the worlds

unimagined by the writer himself.

Resting myself on the edge of their expanse,

I wrestled if I should dive in.

The unknown pulled at me

daring me into its depths.

Existing in that in-betweenness

I thought of the tiny burbling brook

that had now become the ocean,

and I knew,

to see the oyster bring forth the pearl,

I had to become the ocean myself.

And I took the plunge....!

I let in Some Sunshine

I opened the door,

to let in some sunshine.

The picture of many possibilities warmed my heart.

Isn't there always more than meets the eye?

Closing my eyes,

I explored the beauty

the gold of the rays

permeating through my skin

bringing me alive.

Each pore of my being

was ready to discover

the magic,

the miracle called life.

In that one epiphanous instant

I heard the stillness of the moment

the time throbbing through existence

and I

pervading through it all!!

My Daughter

I wonder how she sleeps

the little cherub lost in her dreams

drunk on her world's tiny pleasures

her cup of life brims beyond measures.

Her baby's world curious and keen

Eager to find what is yet unfelt and unseen.

Lying in her crib

a smile lights her sleeping face.

It makes me envy the ease of her being

her miniature world,

colossal in its ways,

beyond my reach.

Her sparkling eyes eloquent,

her gibberish better than my speech,

awakened me from slumber adulthood leads us into,

'm grateful for the lessons her childhood doth teach.

The Miracle

She had just come into being

my tired body untired of looking

at my tiny grand miracle.

Snuggled in the warmth of my labored arms

her dreamy eyes peered at me.

She might have been looking for some signs of

semblance to me

when her lips parted in recognition.

I think I heard the wisdom

when she smiled:

'Oh mother,

What a wonder it is to be,

I am you and you are me!'

Who is the Teacher?

Holding my hand,

in her unsteady steps

she learns to walk,

tomorrow my dove would've learned to fly

and she would glide the same path.

I would then exult at my master's skills.

But there are times I wonder,

Who is the teacher?

I can't really deny her lessons to me-

of enduring patience

of selfless sacrifice

of humility and devotion

- that help me walk the way of love.

For the Brave Hearts

The north-bound winter wind howls,

furious, blustering,

as clouds conceal the sky.

The sun hurtles

intermittently

through the windswept clangour.

And I venture out,

to pick up

the scarce, scattered sun rays

from the choppy ground.

One by one,

I gather the beams of light,

I collect them all;

and fill my quiver

with hope and happiness.

This terra firma is only for the brave hearts!

Wanderlust

Wanderlust

afflicts me

and

the seeker in me

seeks;

and,

the voyage outside

becomes

a pilgrimage within,

a journey to thee!

What Am I?

What am I?

A tiny drop

in

the mighty ocean

of life,

enfeebled by fear

strengthened

when I strive.

The infinity of the sky,

and the abyss of space,

makes me ask

the existential question,

of the meaning

this life serves.

I desire

self-revelation

destined for me.

The Travelled World

The world

I have travelled

lives

in sunny places

within me;

and

I,

become a shrine

of the truth

and the wisdom

of an existence,

earthly,

metaphysical

and divine,

all at once.

You Know Not Me

You know not me
but I exist.

I exist
as a breeze
that refreshes you
when
on the rutted highway
you inadvertently digress.

I exist
as the warmth
in the fire you kindle
all alone
in the darkness of
vernal wilderness.

I exist
as the stomp
in your step
when anger seethes

inside
in a bloody mess.

I exist
as the water
in the lonely brook
that cools
your parched throat
with a maternal caress.

I exist
as a dream
that baffles you
with its proximity
and yet
it eludes the atoning redress.

I exist within you
but you know not me.

By the Ganges

I sit by the Ganges

my feet dipped

in its cool, glacial waters.

I am entranced

by its mightiness,

its formidable power,

and the terrains

it might have crossed

to reach

where I sit

and

the devotees

dip in its holiness

wishing their sins away.

One day

I too will come

to drown in you

when I die

and am dust and ashes

to become

a part of you

a part of

the timelessness

the perpetuity

the infiniteness

that is you!

Under the Chestnut Tree

On a grassy knoll

under the chestnut tree

I sit meditating

on the world

rushing and gushing

in a weird, maddening spree.

Those few hours of quiet,

one bubble of a moment,

a crack, a breakthrough,

for me to see,

what goes into

making and breaking

of you and me,

and all those wondrous journeys,

of love and learning,

on which we are yet to be.

The Whirlwind

The whirlwind inside
tosses me around
for I have probed too long
and still search
for the eternal fountain
of wisdom.

Each time
that I feel I have arrived,
a little bump
sends me rolling back to the start,
and I am forever there,
starting at the start-
A crushing defeat! Alas!

I hope for the day
when this whirlwind
makes me a dervish
and I dance and whirl
reaching back to you!

Darkness

Look,

how at night

we fear

the darkness

inside a room;

but then,

what of the darkness

inside of our heart

that outstrips reason

like the sun eclipsed

in broad daylight!

Epilogue

So, how was your journey through this book of poetry? I don't know if you have read through each page to reach here or you have turned the pages absentmindedly skimming through the pages to reach the end (though I so wish for the former to be true), but in a hope to give this journey a finishing touch I wanted to share something more with you. I wish that you have, on a certain plain, been able to connect with my schmaltzy spirit and that my poems have found a kindred soul in you. Have you ever felt like a photograph, immune to the passage of time, looking at the world pass by you? And have you sometimes found a memory standing and waiting for you at an unexpected turn of life? There is some sense in the contrariety of thought, however confusing and mindboggling it may seem in the beginning. I believe that my solitudinarian sufferance has found way into the minutiae of phenomena around me and I have found my soul pervading through the universe and the soul of the cosmos throbbing within me.

You might think why I am sharing this with you? Perhaps I need you to locate that place inside your heart, akin to the little place inside mine where these poems have come from.

Wishing you pure love and precious hope!

Thank you!!

www.ingramcontent.com/pod-product-compliance
Lightning Source LLC
Chambersburg PA
CBHW031437150726
47989CB00002B/963